Facts About the Giraffe

By Lisa Strattin

© 2019 Lisa Strattin

Facts for Kids Picture Books by Lisa Strattin

Little Blue Penguin, Vol 92

Chipmunk, Vol 5

Frilled Lizard, Vol 39

Blue and Gold Macaw, Vol 13

Poison Dart Frogs, Vol 50

Blue Tarantula, Vol 115

African Elephants, Vol 8

Amur Leopard, Vol 89

Sabre Tooth Tiger, Vol 167

Baboon, Vol 174

Sign Up for New Release Emails Here

http://LisaStrattin.com/subscribe-here

Monthly Surprise Box

http://KidCraftsByLisa.com

Contents

INTRODUCTION

The Giraffe is a long-necked, hoofed mammal that is native to the open woodlands of sub-Saharan Africa. It is the tallest living animal on land.

There are nine recognized sub-species of the giraffe found in different areas. These vary in the color and spot-type markings. Today they are extinct from much of their historically vast native range with only small, isolated populations remaining in a few areas in central Africa. Further south however, the populations are stable and even increasing.

CHARACTERISTICS

The large size of the giraffe means that spends a lot of time eating. During the hottest part of the day, giraffes rest in shady areas. Small herds made up of a number of females and their young spend all of their time together in order to protect their offspring from predators. However, the males are more solitary, they often roam over large regions looking for a female to mate. If they come across a rival male, the two will bump heads and interlock their necks. This is to establish dominance, with the winner of the confrontation earning the right to mate with the females in the area.

APPEARANCE

The giraffe uses the long neck to eat the leaves and vegetation that are too high up for other animals to reach. Despite their length of their neck, it actually contains the same number of bones as many other hoofed mammals. The giraffe has a short body, with long, thin, straight legs and a black tuft tipped long tail that it uses to flip flies away. Giraffes are generally white with brown or reddish markings that cover its body, all except for its lower legs. The markings of each giraffe are unique to that individual and vary greatly between the 9 different species in size, color, and the amount of white that surrounds the spots. Giraffes have large eyes, that along with their height, giving them an excellent view of the surrounding area. They also have small horn-like features on the top of their head.

LIFE STAGES

Giraffes breed year round and once they have found a female to mate, the male goes back to living alone. Gestation lasts for 15 months, then she gives birth to a single infant (twins are rare) that stands at over 6 feet tall and has its own unique markings.

Giraffe calves look just like the adults, simply growing bigger and more elongated as they get older. After birth, the female will keep her calf away from the others of the herd for about 15 days. The calf will be weaned when it is just over one year old.

Males are not always successful breeding until they are nearly eight years old. Although both male and female young will join small groups, the males become more solitary with age, while the females remain in herds with other females and calves.

INTERESTING FACTS

Even though they feed higher than any other animal, males will eat at higher levels than the females do in order to avoid competing with each other for food. If danger is sighted, they will instantly sprint away, running at speeds of more than 30 miles per hour for short periods of time.

Giraffes must go from a walking pace to running, without being able to trot first. They can see for great distances and have a great range of vision, likely the most of any animal that lives exclusively on land.

SIZE

Ad adult giraffe can grow to be as tall at 20 feet and weigh between 1,200 to 4,300 pounds!

HABITAT

Previously found even in North Africa, today the populations are restricted to parts of sub-Saharan Africa.The largest concentrations of them being found in National Parks. The nine species are found in different countries on the African continent, each living within their local region, eating the vegetation native there. Because they eat vegetation that is very high in the trees and too woody for smaller herbivores, they are also able to live in areas where domestic grazing has already removed the plants close to the ground. So there might not be smaller, grazing animals in the same areas because the food is too scarce for them to survive.

DIET

They are herbivores and are known to eat up to 60 different plants throughout the year. They do this by grabbing onto branches with their long, black tongue (that can grow up to 18 inches long) and then using their tough lips and flattened, grooved teeth, they are able to strip the leaves off the branches.

Giraffes most commonly eat from acacia trees but also will look for wild apricots, flowers, fruits and buds, as well as eating seeds and fresh grass just after it rains in their regions. They get most of their moisture from food so need to drink very little water. When they do find a clean water source, they have to spread out their front legs, which are longer than the back legs, in order to get their head close enough to the ground to drink it.

FRIENDS AND ENEMIES

Despite giraffes being the tallest land animal in the world, it is preyed upon by a number of large meat eaters that live along with it in the dry savannah. Lions are the most feared predators of the Giraffe because they use the strength of the whole pride to catch their victim. However, they are also preyed upon by leopards and hyenas. Giraffes kick an attacker with large, heavy feet in order to defend themselves. Young calves however, are much weaker and rely on the mother and herd to protect them. About half of all young giraffes do not make it past the age of 6 months due to the predators.

SUITABILITY AS PETS

It is probably obvious that you could not really keep a giraffe as a pet. Not only are they just too large, but it would be difficult to keep the right kind of tall trees to feed them the food they need to do well. You can see them at most zoos, though, so you can visit them and see them there.

COLOR ME

COLOR ME

COLOR ME

COLOR ME

COLOR ME

COLOR ME

COLOR ME

COLOR ME

COLOR ME

COLOR ME

Please leave me a review here:

http://lisastrattin.com/Review-Vol-197

For more Kindle Downloads Visit Lisa Strattin Author Page on Amazon Author Central

http://amazon.com/author/lisastrattin

To see upcoming titles, visit my website at LisaStrattin.com– all books available on kindle!

http://lisastrattin.com

PLUSH GIRAFFE TOY

You can get one by copying and pasting this link into your browser:

http://lisastrattin.com/PlushGiraffe

MONTHLY SURPRISE BOX

Get yours by copying and pasting this link into your browser

http://KidCraftsByLisa.com

Made in the USA
Monee, IL
19 April 2022

95011238R00024